A Slow Walk with John

A Slow Walk with John

120 Devotional Meditations on 1 John, 2 John, and 3 John

Edward B. Allen

Melbourne

A Slow Walk with John:
120 Devotional Meditations on 1 John, 2 John, and 3 John
by Edward B. Allen
Copyright © 2023 by Edward B. Allen
Reprinted with revisions 2026.
All rights reserved worldwide.

Published by Edward B. Allen
Melbourne, Florida
Email: edward.allen1949@gmail.com

ISBN: 979-8-9875875-3-9 (paperback)
979-8-9875875-4-6 (standard ebook *.epub)
979-8-9875875-5-3 (Kindle ebook)

Contact the publisher if you have questions regarding copying this book.

Scripture quotations marked CSB have been taken from the *Christian Standard Bible*® Copyright © 2017, 2020 by Holman Bible Publishers. Used by permission. *Christian Standard Bible*® and CSB ® are federally registered trademarks of Holman Bible Publishers.

Scriptures quoted in this work are noted by the following abbreviations.

>CSB, *Christian Standard Bible*, © 2017, 2020 Holman Bible Publishers
>KJV, *The Holy Bible, King James Version*, pubic domain

Cover design by Raney Day Creative, LLC.

To Angie

Contents

Preface   xiii

Meditations on 1 John
1	Truth	2
2	Word of life	3
3	Fellowship	4
4	Joy	5
5	Light	6
6	Walking in darkness	7
7	Walking in light	8
8	Deceived	9
9	Forgiven	10
10	Sinner	11
11	Advocate	12
12	Atoning sacrifice	13
13	How to know God	14
14	Pretending to know God	15
15	Love made complete	16
16	Walking	17
17	Already received	18
18	Jesus' new command	19
19	In the dark	20
20	In the light	21

Contents

21	Blind	22
22	To little children	23
23	To fathers	24
24	To young men	25
25	Loving the world	26
26	Desiring the world	27
27	Temporary desires	28
28	Many antichrists	29
29	Belonging	30
30	Anointing	31
31	Knowing the truth	32
32	Denying Jesus	33
33	Confessing the Son	34
34	The Word remaining	35
35	Eternity	36
36	Deceivers	37
37	Taught by the anointing	38
38	Not ashamed	39
39	Doing right	40
40	God's children	41
41	Like him	42
42	Purified	43
43	Lawlessness	44
44	Taking away sin	45
45	Does not keep on sinning	46
46	Righteous	47
47	Destroying the devil's works	48
48	Not practicing sin	49
49	The devil's children	50
50	Love one another	51
51	Unlike Cain	52
52	Hated by the world	53
53	From death to life	54

Contents

54	Murder	55
55	Selfless love	56
56	Love in action	57
57	Assurance	58
58	Confidence	59
59	Believing	60
60	Remaining	61
61	Testing spirits	62
62	Spirit of God	63
63	Spirit of antichrist	64
64	Greater than deception	65
65	From the world	66
66	Who to listen to	67
67	Love is from God	68
68	God is love	69
69	Love revealed	70
70	Sent his Son	71
71	We must love	72
72	Complete love	73
73	Holy Spirit in us	74
74	God sent a Savior	75
75	Son of God	76
76	Knowing God's love	77
77	Remaining in love	78
78	Confidence on judgment day . . .	79
79	No fear	80
80	Loved first	81
81	Loving whom seen	82
82	Born of God	83
83	Obeying God's commands	84
84	Victory	85
85	Conquerer	86
86	Confirmation	87

87	Testimony	88
88	Rejecting testimony	89
89	Life in Jesus	90
90	Eternal life	91
91	Confidence in prayer	92
92	Answers to prayer	93
93	Intercession for believers	94
94	Deadly sin	95
95	Not sinning	96
96	Evil one	97
97	True God	98
98	No idols	99

Meditations on 2 John

99	Eternal truth	102
100	Grace, mercy, and peace	103
101	Walking in truth	104
102	Reminder	105
103	Walking in love	106
104	Many deceivers	107
105	Watch	108
106	Going beyond	109
107	Hospitality	110
108	Greetings from far away	111

Meditations on 3 John

109	Prospering	114
110	Fidelity	115
111	Children walking	116
112	Faithful hospitality	117
113	Supporting evangelists	118
114	Coworkers	119
115	Loving first place	120

Contents

116	Refusing hospitality	121
117	Imitating good	122
118	Good reputation	123
119	Face to face	124
120	Friends	125

Index   **127**

About the author   **133**

Preface

John, the son of Zebedee, was one of Jesus' closest disciples. According to tradition, he lived in Ephesus in his later years and wrote three letters which have been embraced by Christians as part of the Bible. The letters are designated 1 John, 2 John, and 3 John. John wrote about a wide variety of topics including truth, love for one another, the humanity and divinity of Jesus, hospitality, and warning of false teaching.

This book is a collection of devotional meditations, slowly walking through the letters from John a verse or two at a time. The stories are based on the recollections of actual people and events by friends, family, or myself, unless otherwise indicated. Write your personal thoughts about the passage in the blank space at the bottom of most pages.

The *Christian Standard Bible* (CSB) is quoted as the primary translation of the Bible. It is a modern translation based on the latest evangelical scholarship. Clarifications of quotes are in [brackets]. Scripture references consist of book, chapter, verses, and version (if relevant), for example, "1 John 1:1 (CSB)." Cross-references to other Scriptures are in

Preface

the notes. Transliterated Greek words are in *italics*, mostly in notes. Greek definitions are from Strong's *Exhaustive Concordance of the Bible*. Strong's reference numbers for Greek words are used rather than full citations, for example, "(*Strong's* No. 25)." Some background comes from commentaries by Glenn W. Barker,[1] who was an evangelical Bible scholar. All titles and Scripture references are indexed. A word or phrase referred to as a word is in *italics*. Male pronouns are sometimes used to indicate a person of either gender.

I thank my many Facebook friends for their encouraging responses to my series of devotional meditations. I am also thankful for the support of my wife, Angie.

E.B.A.

---

[1] Glenn W. Barker, "1 John," "2 John," and "3 John," *The Expositor's Bible Commentary*, Vol. 12 (Grand Rapids, Michigan: Zondervan, 1981).

Meditations on 1 John

Although John did not identify himself by name in his gospel nor in his letters, church tradition has always attributed these books of the New Testament to John, the son of Zebedee.

1 John 1:1

1 Truth

> What was from the beginning, what we have heard, what we have seen with our eyes, what we have observed and have touched with our hands, concerning the word of life.
>
> 1 John 1:1 (CSB)

John knew Jesus personally and was an eye witness of his resurrection. He heard Jesus preach. He saw Jesus heal the sick and cast out demons. He was close enough to touch Jesus, and to verify he is a human being. John was qualified to tell us Jesus embodies the message of life for us.

Truthfulness used to be important to newspapers and TV news, but in recent years, they seem more interested in their own opinions. When someone tells me a story, I want to know if he is telling the unbiased truth or just fiction. I can trust John to tell the truth about Jesus and his message of life for me.

> PRAYER: Lord, help me to recognize the truth and like John, to always speak the truth to others. Amen.

PERSONAL THOUGHTS

2 Word of life

> That life was revealed, and we have seen it and we testify and declare to you the eternal life that was with the Father and was revealed to us.
>
> 1 John 1:2 (CSB)

John's experience proved Jesus is the source of the life God intended. John wrote to us about eternal life which is available to us through faith in Jesus. A life rebelling against God misses out on a fulfilling relationship with the creator of the universe.

When I was ten years old, I invited Jesus into my life. I welcomed the word of life taught by John's gospel and letters. I knew John's testimony is reliable because he was an eye witness of Jesus' life and resurrection. John's gospel and letters confirmed that I have eternal life.

> PRAYER: Lord, thank you for eternal life with you. Amen.

PERSONAL THOUGHTS

1 John 1:3

3 Fellowship

> What we have seen and heard we also declare to you, so that you may also have fellowship with us; and indeed our fellowship is with the Father and with his Son, Jesus Christ.
>
> 1 John 1:3 (CSB)

Believing the word of life opens the way for fellowship with God the Father and God the Son, Jesus. Those who have fellowship with the Father and the Son also can easily have fellowship with other believers.

When I meet another believer, we have instant rapport. For example, I notice when someone uses a phrase only Christians use. Our relationship with the Lord affects our attitudes, speech, and actions. We don't have to be at church to find out we both know Jesus. We may be in the grocery store aisle or standing in line. Sharing the most important thing in life is our bond.

> PRAYER: Lord, thank you for fellowship with you and with other believers. Amen.

PERSONAL THOUGHTS

4 Joy

> We are writing these things so that our joy may be complete.
>
> 1 John 1:4 (CSB)

John wrote his letter so believers would experience fellowship with God and with each other. A relationship with the Father and the Son removes interference by sin and supplies contentment. John was participating in that fellowship. The result was joy for John and for us, the believers.

My joy is more than happiness due to pleasant surroundings or circumstances. My joy wells up from deep inside me, no matter what the circumstances are. Fellowship with believers confirms what I sense in my soul, because they are God's children.

> PRAYER: Lord, thank you for joy that comes from fellowship with you and your children. Amen.

PERSONAL THOUGHTS

5 Light

> This is the message we have heard from [Jesus] and declare to you: God is light, and there is absolutely no darkness in him.
>
> 1 John 1:5 (CSB)

People use darkness to hide sin. They try to hide sin any way they can, "sweeping it under the rug." Light reveals sin. God doesn't need a flashlight to see under my "rug." He is not fooled by my darkness. He sees everything as in the light. He has no sin and no darkness.

When I was a boy, we sang the hymn "Holy, holy, holy, Lord God Almighty." The first definition I learned for the word *holy* was "without sin." God is not like people. He is holy. When I found out God could see everything I do, even in the dark, I suddenly became much more cautious. I didn't want to do anything to upset him.

> PRAYER: Lord, I still don't want to sin. I know it would displease you. Amen.

PERSONAL THOUGHTS

6 Walking in darkness

> If we say, "We have fellowship with [God]," and yet we walk in darkness, we are lying and are not practicing the truth.
>
> 1 John 1:6 (CSB)

A religious person may claim to be a friend of God. He thinks looking reverent, doing church activities, and contributing money must mean God likes him. However, if he tries to hide his sin in a dark corner, his life is a lie.

It was pitch dark late one night on a camping trip. Everyone was asleep and the campfire had gone out, but I needed to use the latrine. I pretended to know where it was as I stumbled through the woods, but I was lying. Hiding my sin is like stumbling in the dark.

> PRAYER: Lord, I admit that I can't hide my sin from you. Amen.

PERSONAL THOUGHTS

7 Walking in light

> If we walk in the light as [God] himself is in the light, we have fellowship with one another, and the blood of Jesus his Son cleanses us from all sin.
>
> 1 John 1:7 (CSB)

If I will live honestly about my weaknesses and sin, then God will completely forgive. Jesus paid the penalty for my sin when he died on the cross. When I am forgiven by God and honest with others, the door is open for healthy relationships with other believers.

My wife and I have been walking around the block for some exercise. We go along hand-in-hand without tripping on broken sidewalks. Our conversation flows smoothly because we have both been forgiven by God.

> PRAYER: Lord, thank you for cleansing me of all my sin. Amen.

PERSONAL THOUGHTS

1 John 1:8

8 Deceived

> If we say, "We have no sin," we are deceiving ourselves, and the truth is not in us.
>
> 1 John 1:8 (CSB)

If I claim I do not have a sin-prone nature, I am just fooling myself. I can't be honest with God and others if I can't be honest with myself. Refusing to recognize the truth about myself colors my view of all around me.

When I was little, I tried to be a good boy, but sometimes I messed up. I thought trying to be a good boy would get me into heaven. I found out no one is good enough, but Jesus is the answer to my sin-prone nature.

> PRAYER: Lord, I need you to overcome my sin-prone nature. I can't do it myself. Amen.

PERSONAL THOUGHTS

1 John 1:9

9 Forgiven

> If we confess our sins, [God] is faithful and righteous to forgive us our sins and to cleanse us from all unrighteousness.
> 1 John 1:9 (CSB)

When I recognize I have sinned, the solution is to confess to God. He has promised to forgive me and to clean me up.

Sinning is sometimes like a little kid dressed in Sunday best playing at the edge of a puddle. Oops! Suddenly, there is mud on everything. My heavenly Father is like the wise parent who cleans up the foolish kid.

> PRAYER: Lord, thank you for forgiving me every time I fall down. Amen.

PERSONAL THOUGHTS

10 Sinner

> If we say, "We have not sinned," we make [God] a liar, and his word is not in us.
>
> 1 John 1:10 (CSB)

God's Word teaches that everyone has sinned. I am included in *everyone*. If I pretend I'm perfect, in effect, I'm calling God a liar and I am ignoring what the Bible clearly teaches.

"For all have sinned, and come short of the glory of God,"[2] was one of the first Bible verses I memorized in Sunday School. It was obvious I was a sinner no matter how hard I tried to be good. Then I memorized more verses about God's forgiveness.

> PRAYER: Lord, I know that I have sinned ever since I can remember. Thank you for your forgiveness. Amen.

PERSONAL THOUGHTS

---

[2] Romans 3:23 (KJV).

1 John 2:1

11 Advocate

> My little children, I am writing you these things so that you may not sin. But if anyone does sin, we have an advocate with the Father—Jesus Christ the righteous one.
>
> 1 John 2:1 (CSB)

John's letter helps me adjust my life, so I don't sin. But if I do sin, forgiveness is available because Jesus is my advocate. He died, rose from the dead, and ascended into heaven to be next to God the Father.

Becoming a believer did not automatically change my thought patterns and behavior. Sometimes I sin. The Holy Spirit is molding my character, so I have new thought patterns and behavior. Whenever I do sin, Jesus talks to God the Father about me. I have access to God's forgiveness.

> PRAYER: Lord, thank you for being my advocate, so I can be forgiven whenever I need it. Amen.

PERSONAL THOUGHTS

1 John 2:2

12 Atoning sacrifice

> [Jesus] himself is the atoning sacrifice for our sins, and not only for ours, but also for those of the whole world.
> 1 John 2:2 (CSB)

In Old Testament times, certain sacrifices of animals were for paying the price for sin and gaining forgiveness. Animal sacrifices were only a foreshadowing of what was needed. Jesus' death on the cross was the ultimate atoning sacrifice that paid the penalty for all the sin of everyone of all time.

When I became a believer, I didn't understand much from the Bible. I started reading the Bible every day, even the boring parts about Old Testament sacrifices. As I learned about the significance of Jesus' death on the cross, I realized what a wonderful thing Jesus voluntarily did.

> PRAYER: Lord, thank you for paying the price for my sins and that of everyone. Amen.

PERSONAL THOUGHTS

1 John 2:3

13 How to know God

> This is how we know that we know [God]: if we keep his commands.
>
> 1 John 2:3 (CSB)

John was in the inner circle of Jesus' disciples. He knew Jesus personally. John said it is simple to know God personally today: do what he says to do.

When I read the gospels, I see Jesus' instructions. They reveal God's character. Just reading about them is not the same as knowing him personally. His instructions involve the heart, mind, emotions, and actions. Putting them into practice lets me experience the results. Obedience opens the way for the Holy Spirit to interact with me, and then I know God personally.

> PRAYER: Lord, thank you for letting me know you personally. Amen.

PERSONAL THOUGHTS

1 John 2:4

14 Pretending to know God

> The one who says, "I have come to know [God]," and yet doesn't keep his commands, is a liar, and the truth is not in him.
>
> 1 John 2:4 (CSB)

If I claim to know God personally, but do not obey his instructions, then I am just pretending to know him.

Claiming to know God after only sitting in church and listening to a sermon, is like the person who claims to know a movie star because he saw a movie and read an article in a magazine. Many people do religious things but do not obey Jesus' instructions. They miss out on interaction with the Holy Spirit in daily life.

> PRAYER: Lord, I don't want to just pretend to know you. Amen.

PERSONAL THOUGHTS

1 John 2:5

15   Love made complete

> But whoever keeps [God's] word, truly in him the love of God is made complete.
>
> 1 John 2:5 (CSB)

God's love for me is something I can sense. When I love others, I sense God's love for them. "Keeping God's word" means obeying his instructions. When I do this, God's love is expressed in my actions.

In modern culture, the word *love* has a vague meaning. Many associate it only with sex between two people. Some think of relationships in a family or between close friends. Jesus sacrificed himself so I can be free from sin's ultimate consequence—death. What Jesus did is evidence of God's love for mankind. When I follow his instructions, I am expressing God's love for people.

> PRAYER: Lord, I will keep your word so that your love will be expressed through my actions. Amen.

PERSONAL THOUGHTS

1 John 2:5–6

16 Walking

> This is how we know we are in [Christ]:
> The one who says he remains in him
> should walk just as [Jesus] walked.
> 1 John 2:5–6 (CSB)

Believers are "in Christ."[3] They are in the Body of Christ like a hand is in a person's body. How can I know that I am in Christ? The evidence is living my life the same way Jesus did. He obeyed God the Father's commands.

When I was a Boy Scout, we learned to march in formation like soldiers. We all took a step at the same time with the same foot. We learned to pivot for "left face," "right face," and "about face." We had to listen carefully for the leader's commands. Walking like Jesus means putting into practice what the gospels teach, and by listening for the Holy Spirit.

> PRAYER: Lord, help me be sensitive to your instructions throughout each day. Amen.

PERSONAL THOUGHTS

---

[3] For example, John 15:4–5 and Romans 8:1.

1 John 2:7

17 Already received

> Dear friends, I am not writing you a new command but an old command that you have had from the beginning. The old command is the word you have heard.
> 1 John 2:7 (CSB)

John emphasized that his teaching in this letter was not advocating something new. It was the same gospel his readers had already received.

The teaching of the New Testament is consistent, even though the books were written by eight authors[4] for various recipients over a span of decades for various situations. John's letter reinforces what I have learned ever since the Sunday School classes of my childhood.

> PRAYER: Lord, thank you for inspiring godly men to write the New Testament for believers like me. Amen.

PERSONAL THOUGHTS

---

[4] Assuming Paul wrote Hebrews.

1 John 2:8

18 Jesus' new command

> Yet I am writing you a new command, which is true in [Jesus] and in you, because the darkness is passing away and the true light is already shining.
>
> 1 John 2:8 (CSB)

Jesus gave his disciples a new command, "Just as I have loved you, you are also to love one another."[5] In this letter, John is passing this command on to us.

Jesus demonstrated his love for us by sacrificing his life on the cross. My love for other believers should be self-sacrificing also. When we have unselfish lives, the light of the gospel shines.

> PRAYER: Lord, help me live with self-sacrificing love all the time. Amen.

PERSONAL THOUGHTS

---

[5]John 13:34 (CSB). The Greek word *agapao* (*Strong's* No. 25) is translated as "love" throughout John's letters and means the kind of self-sacrificing love Jesus had. Other Greek words mean brotherly love and sexual love.

1 John 2:9

19   In the dark

> The one who says he is in the light but hates his brother or sister is in the darkness until now.
>
> 1 John 2:9 (CSB)

If I hate my fellow believer, then I am living in spiritual darkness. Pretending to be a good Christian while hating a fellow believer proves I don't know what I'm talking about.

Throughout church history, there have been schisms. Believers have hated one another over theology, tradition, or leadership. Some believers have mistaken ideas about theology. Some leaders may be incompetent or corrupt. Believers sin sometimes. People use these as excuses for anger, hatred, and bitterness, which result in spiritual darkness.

> PRAYER: Lord, correct me whenever I turn toward anger, hatred, and bitterness. I confess I'm weak. Amen.

PERSONAL THOUGHTS

1 John 2:10

20   In the light

> The one who loves his brother or sister remains in the light, and there is no cause for stumbling in him.
> 1 John 2:10 (CSB)

Self-sacrificing love is the antidote to anger, hatred, and bitterness. When one walks in the light, the way ahead is clear. That believer won't stumble into sin.

Angie noticed a Christian sister at church seemed offended. Angie apologized even though she didn't know why the sister was offended. By a week later, all was resolved without a big discussion.

When I have offended a fellow believer, finding a practical way to express my love usually resolves the relationship. I may find a creative way to be helpful. Another believer may bring us together. We both need to stay in the light.

> PRAYER: Lord, I am determined to love my fellow believers. Help me avoid stumbling. Amen.

PERSONAL THOUGHTS

1 John 2:11

21 Blind

> But the one who hates his brother or sister is in the darkness, walks in the darkness, and doesn't know where he's going, because the darkness has blinded his eyes.
>
> 1 John 2:11 (CSB)

Living with hatred is like walking in the dark. One is easily disoriented. One is easily deceived. Hatred blinds one to reality.

When I was a kid, we played "pin the tail on the donkey." I would be blindfolded and spun around and around. I was then supposed to pin the tail in my hand onto a picture of a donkey. Everyone else was shouting directions, which weren't very helpful. Hatred in my heart is just as dark as a blindfold and just as futile as "pin the tail on the donkey."

> PRAYER: Lord, help me prevent hatred from blinding me. Amen.

PERSONAL THOUGHTS

1 John 2:12–14

22 To little children

> I am writing to you, little children,
> since your sins have been forgiven
> on account of [Jesus'] name...
> I have written to you, children,
> because you have come to know the Father...
>
> 1 John 2:12–14 (CSB)

Verses 12 through 14 is a poetic passage commending three categories of believers: little children, fathers, and young men. *Little children* can refer to anyone who is a new believer irrespective of physical age. *Fathers* can refer to the spiritually mature. *Young men* also applies to young women. Each group is addressed twice.

When I believed in Jesus, God adopted me into his spiritual family. I became his child. I didn't know much about the Christian life, but I knew my sins were forgiven and I could personally talk with God. I could honestly pray, "Our Father..."

> PRAYER: Lord, thank you for including me in your spiritual family. Amen.

PERSONAL THOUGHTS

1 John 2:13–14

23 To fathers

> I am writing to you, fathers,
> because you have come to know
> the one who is from the beginning…
> I have written to you, fathers,
> because you have come to know
> the one who is from the beginning…
> 1 John 2:13–14 (CSB)

John repeated his commendation of fathers to emphasize the importance of knowing the Creator. Experiences in the faith over the years are foundations for understanding the Creator's ways and for forming a deep intimate relationship with him.

Relationships with people I've known a long time are built on our many shared experiences. I don't just know about them. I know them well in a personal way. Spending time with God in prayer, Bible reading, and meditation has built my relationship with him.

> PRAYER: Lord, thank you for letting me know you personally. Amen.

PERSONAL THOUGHTS

1 John 2:13–14

24 To young men

> I am writing to you, young men,
> because you have conquered the evil one...
> I have written to you, young men,
> because you are strong,
> God's word remains in you,
> and you have conquered the evil one.
> 1 John 2:13–14 (CSB)

Believers who are strong in the faith are able to defeat Satan's schemes. Knowing God's Word is their essential weapon. In John's vision in Revelation, they overcame Satan by the blood of Jesus and their testimony, even risking death.[6]

Knowing what the Bible says has been important in my spiritual walk. God's Word equips me to properly respond to circumstances the world throws at me. I know I have the authority of Jesus. He has all power because he died for me and rose from the dead.

> PRAYER: Lord, thank you for your Word which gives me strength in difficult circumstances. Amen.

PERSONAL THOUGHTS

---

[6] Revelation 12:11.

1 John 2:15

25 Loving the world

> Do not love the world or the things in the world. If anyone loves the world, the love of the Father is not in him.
> 1 John 2:15 (CSB)

John said not to love the world. The word *world* here refers to human life: lifestyles, things, systems, and institutions. Unbelievers measure success in terms of such things. What do I consider to be most important: loving human level things or the heavenly Father?

Like everyone else, I live on a human level dealing with food, shelter, clothing, a job and so on. As a believer, I also live in the kingdom of God. My affections, energy, and ambitions can be directed toward all the details of daily life on a human level or directed toward the heavenly Father. If I seek first the kingdom of God, my heavenly Father will provide all the mundane things I need.[7]

> PRAYER: Lord, I choose to give you priority over things of this world. Amen.

PERSONAL THOUGHTS

---

[7] Matthew 6:33.

1 John 2:16

26 Desiring the world

> For everything in the world—the lust of the flesh, the lust of the eyes, and the pride in one's possessions—is not from the Father, but is from the world.
>
> 1 John 2:16 (CSB)

What the world offers is summarized by human desires, envy, and pride. These are not the godly desires of living in the kingdom of God. They are corrupt and worldly.

When I first saw this verse as a teenager, I was shocked, because all my friends were driven by lust, envy, and pride, and I thought they were okay. I found out that pleasing the heavenly Father is different.

> PRAYER: Lord, I want my life to be pleasing to you. Amen.

PERSONAL THOUGHTS

1 John 2:17

27 Temporary desires

> And the world with its lust is passing away, but the one who does the will of God remains forever.
>
> 1 John 2:17 (CSB)

All the things worldly people wish for are just temporary. Feeding lust, envy, and pride doesn't produce anything of lasting value. Doing what God wants me to do leads to things of eternal value.

The Scriptures teach me how to live as a citizen of the kingdom of God. Obeying the nudges of the Holy Spirit results in amazing coincidences for those around me.

For example, one Friday night I felt an urgency to search my files for the sheet music of a particular song. The next day at church, I played background music for a prayer meeting, so I sang that song first. Just at that moment, a lady came in who had been thinking about that song all week. To her, it was a "sign and a wonder" from God. God was paying attention to her. I was just singing a song.

> PRAYER: Lord, you arrange amazing coincidences. Amen.

PERSONAL THOUGHTS

1 John 2:18

28 Many antichrists

> Children, it is the last hour. And as you have heard that antichrist is coming, even now many antichrists have come. By this we know that it is the last hour.
> 1 John 2:18 (CSB)

John's readers knew that the Antichrist will come on the world scene before Jesus returns. John pointed out there are many opposed to Jesus who are already on the world scene. Therefore, we are in the last hour before Jesus returns.

As a teenager, I was very interested in the second coming of Jesus and all the "signs of the times." His coming is soon. Signs of the last hour have been evident ever since John wrote his letter.[8]

> PRAYER: Lord, I am eagerly waiting for your return to Planet Earth. Amen.

PERSONAL THOUGHTS

---

[8] This letter was written perhaps about AD 90.

1 John 2:19

29 Belonging

> [The antichrists] went out from us, but they did not belong to us; for if they had belonged to us, they would have remained with us. However, they went out so that it might be made clear that none of them belongs to us.
> 1 John 2:19 (CSB)

Ever since John's time, various world leaders have been labeled the "Antichrist." However, another candidate always arises later. Sometimes it is hard to tell who are antichrists. John pointed out if they leave the Christian community, it is evidence the spirit of antichrist is at work.

Ever since I became a believer, I've known belonging to Jesus is different from belonging to this or that church denomination. As I read about church history, I'm saddened by the many schisms and divisions when the spirit of antichrist was at work.

> PRAYER: Lord, show me how I can contribute to unity among believers. Amen.

PERSONAL THOUGHTS

1 John 2:20

30 Anointing

> But you have an anointing from the Holy One, and all of you know the truth.
>
> 1 John 2:20 (CSB)

In Old Testament times, priests and sacred objects were anointed with oil to set them apart for God's service. Similarly, believers are "anointed" with the Holy Spirit. He helps believers distinguish truth from lies.

I was already a believer by the time I went to high school. My English class discussed a novel where the main character was depressed. The class discussion had lots of ideas about his depression. It was obvious to me that the character's sin was why he was depressed. Even in high school, the Holy Spirit helped me recognize the fallacies of worldly wisdom in History, Literature, and Philosophy classes.

> PRAYER: Lord, thank you for sending the Holy Spirit. Amen.

PERSONAL THOUGHTS

1 John 2:21

31 Knowing the truth

> I have not written to you because you don't know the truth, but because you do know it, and because no lie comes from the truth.
>
> 1 John 2:21 (CSB)

Believers know the truth about Jesus. They can detect lies that don't line up with the truth.

I have forgiveness from God because of Jesus. Complex theology can't persuade me of anything different. I know forgiveness is true because I have experienced it, and the gospel explains it.

A wise pastor once said, "The one with an experience is never at the mercy of one with only an argument."

> PRAYER: Lord, thank you for revealing your truth to me. Amen.

PERSONAL THOUGHTS

1 John 2:22

32 Denying Jesus

> Who is the liar, if not the one who denies that Jesus is the Christ? This one is the antichrist: the one who denies the Father and the Son.
> 1 John 2:22 (CSB)

In John's day, a popular heresy denied that Jesus is the Messiah ("Christ" in Greek). John identified the antichrist as those who deny the divinity of Jesus, namely, those denying the Trinity.

I have personally met some who claim Jesus was just a good teacher. They don't want to be confronted by the gospel. They deny Jesus is the Messiah, the Son of God, a person in the Trinity. They are against who Jesus really is, "antichrist."

PRAYER: Lord, give me words to respond to those who deny Jesus. Amen.

PERSONAL THOUGHTS

1 John 2:23

33 Confessing the Son

> No one who denies the Son has the Father; he who confesses the Son has the Father as well.
>
> 1 John 2:23 (CSB)

Because the Trinity is one God, Jesus, the Son of God, is unified with God the Father. Denying the divinity of Jesus, means denying God the Father, too. When I explain that I believe in Jesus, I am also confessing I believe in God the Father, too.

The doctrine of the Trinity has been hard to understand ever since John's day. I don't need to get entangled in the logic of complex theology. By faith, I know who Jesus is and I have an active relationship with God.

> PRAYER: Lord, thank you for forgiving me through faith in Jesus, and for loving me like a father. Amen.
>
> PERSONAL THOUGHTS

34 The Word remaining

> What you have heard from the beginning is to remain in you. If what you have heard from the beginning remains in you, then you will remain in the Son and in the Father.
>
> 1 John 2:24 (CSB)

John emphasized what Jesus taught. Jesus said, "I am the vine; you are the branches. The one who remains in me and I in him produces much fruit."[9]

At the beginning of my Christian walk, I heard the gospel and I responded in faith. I still believe the gospel and my relationship with God has grown deeper. I have seen spiritual fruit as a result, things like love, joy, and peace.

> PRAYER: Lord, thank you for sticking with me through the ups and downs of my spiritual walk. Amen.

PERSONAL THOUGHTS

---

[9] John 15:5 (CSB).

35 Eternity

> And this is the promise that [Jesus] himself made to us: eternal life.
>
> 1 John 2:25 (CSB)

Many times Jesus promised eternal life to those who believe. For example, Jesus said, "Truly I tell you, anyone who hears my word and believes him who sent me has eternal life and will not come under judgment but has passed from death to life."[10]

Eternity is a long time, an infinite length of time. When I studied infinity in Math class, it was hard to imagine. I may not understand infinity very well, but I believed what Jesus said, so I have been forgiven. He has given me eternal life. His life in me has already begun and will last forever. Life with Jesus is much better than what the world offers.

> PRAYER: Lord, thank you for eternal life. Amen.

PERSONAL THOUGHTS

---

[10] John 5:24 (CSB).

1 John 2:26

36 Deceivers

> I have written these things to you concerning those who are trying to deceive you.
>
> 1 John 2:26 (CSB)

The reason John wrote his letter was there will be some who will try to deceive believers about who Jesus is. John warned me about their schemes so I can cling to the truth.

Ever since John's time, deceivers have pushed various false teachings. Reading through the entire New Testament has helped me keep a balanced perspective. (Reading through the Old Testament was challenging.) Knowing what the Bible teaches is my sure defense and I won't be fooled by someone's clever ideas.

> PRAYER: Lord, thank you for your Word, the Bible, which helps me see the truth. Amen.

PERSONAL THOUGHTS

1 John 2:27

37   Taught by the anointing

> As for you, the anointing you received from [God] remains in you, and you don't need anyone to teach you. Instead, his anointing teaches you about all things and is true and is not a lie; just as it has taught you, remain in him.
>
> 1 John 2:27 (CSB)

John used the picture of anointing to illustrate the Holy Spirit in a believer. The Holy Spirit is in me. He teaches me, so I can see the truth. He helps me recognize false ideas about Jesus.

I went with a friend to visit a home Bible study. Most of those present were young people. There was one older lady whom everyone seemed to look up to. As she talked, the Holy Spirit nudged me to keep my guard up, because what she was saying was not quite right. I didn't go back.

> PRAYER: Lord, thank you for the Holy Spirit who guides and teaches me. Amen.

PERSONAL THOUGHTS

1 John 2:28

38   Not ashamed

> So now, little children, remain in [Christ] so that when he appears we may have confidence and not be ashamed before him at his coming.
>
> 1 John 2:28 (CSB)

When Jesus returns, he will know what I've been doing. Will I be ashamed of my attitudes and actions? Remaining in him is the way to stay out of trouble.

A Mom knows when a little one is not making noise, there is mischief in the air. "Eddie, what are you doing?" When Eddie gets caught, he is ashamed. Jesus can see more than Mom. Will I get caught and be ashamed at his coming?

> PRAYER: Lord, I want to remain in you, so I won't be ashamed when you show up. Amen.

PERSONAL THOUGHTS

1 John 2:29

39 Doing right

> If you know that [God] is righteous, you know this as well: Everyone who does what is right has been born of him.
>
> 1 John 2:29 (CSB)

How can I tell if someone is a believer in Jesus? Their words and actions reveal what is in their hearts. For example, an unexpected kindness is a clue that one has been born again.

Angie and Barbara saw a lady in the parking lot who appeared to be sick. After talking with her, they drove her home in her car. After getting home, they made sure a friend would come over to help. She found out by their kindness that they were believers. Do my words and actions demonstrate that I know Jesus?

> PRAYER: Lord, I want to show I belong to you by doing what is right. Amen.

PERSONAL THOUGHTS

1 John 3:1

40 God's children

> See what great love the Father has given us that we should be called God's children—and we are! The reason the world does not know us is that it didn't know him.
>
> 1 John 3:1 (CSB)

God the Father demonstrated his love for mankind by adopting believers into his family. They are called his children. Unbelievers don't know the Father and thus, don't understand believers.

I know several families who have adopted multiple children, some very young and some older, some siblings and some unrelated. Each family had to make each child feel loved and work out the dynamics of a large family. God has a large family too. He has adopted me and many others. When we get together, outsiders don't understand how we love one another.

> PRAYER: Lord, thank you for adopting me to be your child. Amen.

PERSONAL THOUGHTS

1 John 3:2

41 Like him

> Dear friends, we are God's children now, and what we will be has not yet been revealed. We know that when [Jesus] appears, we will be like him because we will see him as he is.
>
> 1 John 3:2 (CSB)

When Jesus was resurrected from the dead, his immortal body was recognizable but different from his old mortal body. The disciples could see the scars from his crucifixion, but he came through a locked door. Paul explained, when Jesus returns, believers will be resurrected into immortal bodies like that of Jesus.[11]

I wonder what my resurrected body will be like. Will I have wings? Probably not. Will I have a white robe? Maybe. I don't know what it will be like, but I know it will be good, because it will be like his. Best of all, I will get to see Jesus with my own eyes.

> PRAYER: Father, thank you for the promise that when Jesus returns I will be like him. Amen.

PERSONAL THOUGHTS

---

[11] 1 Corinthians 15:49–54.

1 John 3:3

42 Purified

> And everyone who has this hope in him purifies himself just as [Jesus] is pure.
> 1 John 3:3 (CSB)

Jesus is sinless; he is pure. He is our example and teacher. Consequently, believers pursue staying out of sin.

I have some rubber boots in my shed for working in the yard. After a rain, they get muddy. I have to rinse them off before I put them away. Whenever I get muddy from sin, I must ask for forgiveness. I have the hope for resurrection, therefore want to keep myself pure. I don't want to need cleaning up when Jesus returns.

> PRAYER: Lord, help me to be pure in all my thoughts and actions. Amen.

PERSONAL THOUGHTS

1 John 3:4

43 Lawlessness

> Everyone who commits sin practices lawlessness; and sin is lawlessness.
> 1 John 3:4 (CSB)

Lawlessness is living in rebellion against the law of God. Rebellion is sin, and sin is a synonym for lawlessness. On the last day, Jesus will judge the lawless and expel them from his presence.[12] John emphasized that sin and lawlessness mean the same thing.

If I live by my opinion of what is right, I am lawless. Selfishness is lawless, because it ignores God's law, and excuses sin. Religious hypocrisy is lawless, because it hides sin under religious rituals. On the last day, there will be no excuses for lawlessness.

> PRAYER: Lord, thank you for forgiving my sins. I will no longer live in rebellion against you. Amen.

PERSONAL THOUGHTS

---

[12] Matthew 7:21–23.

1 John 3:5

44 Taking away sin

> You know that [Jesus] was revealed so that he might take away sins, and there is no sin in him.
>
> 1 John 3:5 (CSB)

Jesus' mission coming to earth was to take away everyone's sin. To do this, he had to live a sinless life to qualify as the perfect sacrifice. Jesus was fully human and was tempted to sin like everyone else, yet without sinning.[13] His trial was a complete injustice; he was innocent of any crime. Yet his crucifixion paid for the sin of mankind.

Garbage accumulates at my house. I have to collect it from each room, put it in my trash can, and take the can to the street. The city takes away everyone's garbage, so the neighborhood is clean. Jesus has taken my sin away, so I am clean.

> PRAYER: Lord, thank you for taking away my sin. Amen.

PERSONAL THOUGHTS

---

[13] Hebrews 4:15.

1 John 3:6

45 Does not keep on sinning

> Everyone who remains in [Jesus] does not keep on sinning; everyone who keeps on sinning[14] has not seen him or known him.
>
> 1 John 3:6 (CSB)

Everyone who has a relationship with Jesus has the power to overcome sin. Those without faith in him don't. Knowing Jesus personally is motivation to avoid sin.

Not only does faith in Jesus result in forgiveness of my past sins, it gives me the ability to stop sinning over and over again.

I used to frequently make cynical jokes. As I matured as a believer, I realized I had to stop. Now that I know Jesus personally, I don't have to sin over and over. I want to please him by not sinning.

> PRAYER: Lord, thank you for the ability to overcome sin, so I don't keep on doing it. Amen.

PERSONAL THOUGHTS

---

[14]Quoting the footnotes of the *Christian Standard Bible* for clarity.

1 John 3:7

46 Righteous

> Little children, let no one deceive you. The one who does what is right is righteous, just as [Jesus] is righteous.
>
> 1 John 3:7 (CSB)

Jesus always did what was right. That is why he is called "righteous." My job as a disciple is to imitate him. People in the world often make excuses for sin, calling evil "good" and good "evil." Clinging to the truth exposes such deception.

There are many examples of how the world twists language. Sexual immorality is called "love." Abortion is called "medical care." Bribery is called "lobbying." A slogan on a tee-shirt is called "violence." A riot is called "mostly peaceful." When I speak, I will just tell the truth.

> PRAYER: Lord, give me your perspective, so I will consistently recognize what is right. Amen.

PERSONAL THOUGHTS

1 John 3:8

47   Destroying the devil's works

> The one who practices[15] sin is of the devil, for the devil has sinned from the beginning. The Son of God was revealed for this purpose: to destroy the devil's works.
>
> 1 John 3:8 (CSB)

A lifestyle of sin is inspired by Satan. When Jesus was on earth, he routinely cast out demons, destroying what the devil had accomplished in victims' lives. His power to do this authenticated his identity as the Son of God.

When I repented of my selfish lifestyle, the devil had lost the war in me. Whenever I help someone repent and turn to Jesus, I am helping destroy the devil's works.

> PRAYER: Lord, show me when I have a role in destroying the devil's works. Amen.

PERSONAL THOUGHTS

---

[15] Quoting the footnote of the *Christian Standard Bible* for clarity.

1 John 3:9

48   Not practicing sin

> Everyone who has been born of God does not practice sin, because his seed remains in him; he is not able to keep on sinning,[16] because he has been born of God.
>
> 1 John 3:9 (CSB)

A believer has been born again by the Spirit, so he does not continue to sin. He has a God-given new nature that hates sin.

Some sinful patterns are compulsive. Submitting to Jesus breaks the power of those patterns. For example, Hansel was an alcoholic, but when he repented and asked Jesus into his life, he never drank alcohol again. He was free.

> PRAYER: Lord, thank you for breaking the power of compulsive sinful patterns. Amen.

PERSONAL THOUGHTS

---

[16] Quoting the footnotes of the *Christian Standard Bible* for clarity.

1 John 3:10

49 The devil's children

> This is how God's children and the devil's children become obvious. Whoever does not do what is right is not of God, especially the one who does not love his brother or sister.
>
> 1 John 3:10 (CSB)

One's actions reveal one's family: God's or the devil's. A pattern of sinning and hating members of God's family indicates one is not in God's family.

All kinds of people are welcome to attend my church. Not everyone who shows up is a mature believer. Some are just immature in the faith. Some are not yet believers but are still seeking the truth. Some pretend to be believers, but their lives and attitudes show which family they belong to.

> PRAYER: Lord, thank you for adopting me into your family. Amen.

PERSONAL THOUGHTS

1 John 3:11

50 Love one another

> For this is the message you have heard from the beginning: We should love one another.
>
> 1 John 3:11 (CSB)

Jesus gave his disciples this command, to love one another like he loves.[17] This command applies to me. There are no excuses.

A wide variety of people are believers. I'm supposed to love them all, even the irritating ones. I can't expect everyone to act like a mature saint. I can't expect everyone to know the Bible. Grace and forgiveness are often needed. We are all learning to walk the Jesus way.

> PRAYER: Lord, I will love all my brothers and sisters, even the cranky ones. Amen.

PERSONAL THOUGHTS

---

[17] John 13:34–35.

1 John 3:12

51 Unlike Cain

> Unlike Cain, who was of the evil one and murdered his brother. And why did he murder him? Because his deeds were evil, and his brother's were righteous.
> 1 John 3:12 (CSB)

Cain and Abel were sons of Adam and Eve. Cain murdered Abel.[18] He did not love his brother. Anyone who hates his Christian brother or sister is like Cain.

I learned the story of Cain and Abel in Sunday School. Ever since, I've known corrupt emotions lead to sinful actions. Acting religious like Cain did does not excuse hating my brother.

> PRAYER: Lord, help me guard my emotions, so I don't fall into sin. Amen.

PERSONAL THOUGHTS

---

[18] Genesis 4:1–16.

1 John 3:13

52 Hated by the world

> Do not be surprised, brothers and sisters, if the world hates you.
> 1 John 3:13 (CSB)

The world hated Jesus. It hates his followers. This gets expressed in many ways: insults, harassment, lawsuits, arrests, jail, death, and so on. The world hates Christians. So I shouldn't be surprised if I'm mistreated.

America has remnants of Western Civilization, which has a Christian heritage, so persecution of Christians is not as explicit as in other places. However, the more the gospel is evident in the lives of Christians, the more the world's hatred comes to the surface.

> PRAYER: Lord, give me your perspective when I am mistreated by worldly people. Amen.

PERSONAL THOUGHTS

1 John 3:14

53 From death to life

> We know that we have passed from death to life because we love our brothers and sisters. The one who does not love remains in death.
>
> 1 John 3:14 (CSB)

What is evidence that one has passed from a lifestyle of death into life in God's kingdom? Loving fellow believers with self-sacrificing love is the evidence.

A lifestyle of death gets expressed in many ways. For example, many of my friends in college abused alcohol. One had to drop out because alcoholism ruined his grades. I can't think of a good reason to stay in a lifestyle of death. Because of Jesus, I have passed from death into life. Loving my fellow believers is a natural result. A pattern of love in action is evidence of my new way of life.

> PRAYER: Lord, thank you for bringing me from death into life. Amen.

PERSONAL THOUGHTS

1 John 3:15

54 Murder

> Everyone who hates his brother or sister is a murderer, and you know that no murderer has eternal life residing in him.
>
> 1 John 3:15 (CSB)

Hatred is morally equivalent to murder. Jesus taught the same thing.[19] This is especially true of hating fellow believers. Sin has eternal consequences.

The physical consequences are not the same for victims of hatred and murder. A victim of murder dies and the murderer goes to jail. The target of hatred goes on with life and may even be unaware. However, for the perpetrator, the moral consequences are the same for both murder and hatred. Sin results in death.

> PRAYER: Lord, guard my heart. Help me to always forgo hatred. Amen.

PERSONAL THOUGHTS

---

[19] Matthew 5:21–22.

1 John 3:16

55 Selfless love

> This is how we have come to know love: [Jesus] laid down his life for us. We should also lay down our lives for our brothers and sisters.
>
> 1 John 3:16 (CSB)

How can I express love? How did Jesus express love? He let men execute him on the cross. I can imitate him by sacrificing selfish desires for the benefit of my fellow believers.

Obviously, I have not yet died for the benefit of a fellow believer, but there are a thousand opportunities to sacrifice my convenience, time, things, or money for others. A simple example is giving someone a ride home which takes me out of my way. Such sacrifices demonstrate love.

PRAYER: Lord, thank you for loving me. Amen.

PERSONAL THOUGHTS

1 John 3:17–18

56 Love in action

> If anyone has this world's goods and sees a fellow believer in need but withholds compassion from him—how does God's love reside in him? Little children, let us not love in word or speech, but in action and in truth.
>
> 1 John 3:17–18 (CSB)

John gives an example of lack of love in actions. Suppose a believer is in need. When a fellow believer who sees this withholds compassion, he is not demonstrating God's love. Love must not be superficial, but must be expressed in acts of kindness.

Boasting about how I love others is usually just hypocrisy. Practical love is patient, kind, not envious, not arrogant, and not selfish.[20] Sometimes creativity is necessary to express kindness to a cranky person.

> PRAYER: Lord, give me a heart of compassion and creative ways to put it into action. Amen.

PERSONAL THOUGHTS

---

[20] 1 Corinthians 13:4–5.

1 John 3:19–20

57   Assurance

> [Love in action] is how we will know that we belong to the truth and will reassure our hearts before him whenever our hearts condemn us; for God is greater than our hearts, and he knows all things.
>
> 1 John 3:19–20 (CSB)

Love in action is evidence that I belong to Jesus. If I feel condemned because of my weaknesses, I can see the love in action that I'm doing because Jesus is in my life. This is reassuring. God's approval is greater than my feelings.

I was a member of a church that had a program every night of the week. If I tried to participate in everything, I would burn out. I felt inadequate. Everyone has times of feeling inadequate compared to God's standard of righteousness. Belonging to Jesus is based on his grace, not my feelings of achievement. Love in action flows naturally when I've experienced God's grace, and is evidence that I belong to him.

> PRAYER: Lord, thank you for assurance, even when I feel inadequate. Amen.

PERSONAL THOUGHTS

1 John 3:21–22

58 Confidence

> Dear friends, if our hearts don't condemn us, we have confidence before God and receive whatever we ask from him because we keep his commands and do what is pleasing in his sight.
> 1 John 3:21–22 (CSB)

When I have assurance that I belong to God's family, I do not feel condemned and I am confident that God will answer my prayers. A lifestyle that does what God likes is rewarding.

I study the Bible to find out what is pleasing to God. I see he likes a loving attitude and righteous actions that express his love for mankind. The Bible also teaches me to pray any time, anywhere, and about anything. When I do what the Bible teaches, he answers my prayers.

> PRAYER: Lord, thank you for confidence that you will answer my prayers. Amen.

PERSONAL THOUGHTS

1 John 3:23

59 Believing

> Now this is [God's] command: that we believe in the name of his Son, Jesus Christ, and love one another as he commanded us.
>
> 1 John 3:23 (CSB)

What does God want from me? It is simple: to have faith in Jesus and to love other believers.

In John's culture, *believe in the name* meant have faith in the person. Jesus is that person, the Messiah. Both the words *Christ* (from Greek) and *Messiah* (from Hebrew) mean anointed one. The Messiah is not only the heir of King David, he is also the Son of God.

The Old Testament teaches me to love my neighbor as I love myself. Jesus teaches me to love other believers in the same way he loves me.[21] Jesus showed he loves me by voluntarily dying on the cross. I must love others with the same self-sacrificing love.

> PRAYER: Lord, my faith is in Jesus and I will do whatever he asks of me. Amen.

PERSONAL THOUGHTS

---

[21] Leviticus 19:18 and John 13:34.

1 John 3:24

60 Remaining

> The one who keeps [Jesus'] commands remains in him, and he in him. And the way we know that he remains in us is from the Spirit he has given us.
> 1 John 3:24 (CSB)

The Holy Spirit in me is evidence that I belong to Jesus. Because I belong to him, I will diligently keep his commands.

I wasn't aware of the Holy Spirit when I believed at ten years old. When I was twelve years old, I heard the whisper of the Holy Spirit as I was reading my Bible. I thought, "Oh, that's what the preacher was talking about." He has been nudging and whispering to me ever since.

> PRAYER: Lord, thank you for the Holy Spirit in me. Amen.

PERSONAL THOUGHTS

1 John 4:1

61 Testing spirits

> Dear friends, do not believe every spirit, but test the spirits to see if they are from God, because many false prophets have gone out into the world.
>
> 1 John 4:1 (CSB)

A prophet will claim to hear from a spirit. A godly prophet hears from the Holy Spirit. A false prophet hears from some other spirit. So when someone prophesies, it is necessary to test the spirit of the prophecy. John warned us that there are many false prophets.

Some churches I have attended are receptive to the gift of prophecy.[22] Sometimes the prophet has a true word from God; sometimes the word is from human wisdom; and sometimes the word is false, contrary to the Bible. Testing the spirit of a prophecy is necessary.

> PRAYER: Lord, thank you for guidance to distinguish true from false prophecy. Amen.

PERSONAL THOUGHTS

---

[22] 1 Corinthians 12:10.

1 John 4:2

62 Spirit of God

> This is how you know the Spirit of God: Every spirit that confesses that Jesus Christ has come in the flesh is from God.
>
> 1 John 4:2 (CSB)

In John's time, there were so-called Christians who claimed Jesus was only a spirit-being who looked like a man. John refuted this doctrine. Jesus had to be an ordinary man for his death on the cross to be meaningful for mankind's forgiveness.

Even today, there are some so-called Christians who either deny Jesus was the divine Son of God or deny he was human. The Bible refutes both of these doctrines. Prophecies that lean in either direction are false.

> PRAYER: Lord, thank you for sending Jesus as an ordinary person. Amen.

PERSONAL THOUGHTS

1 John 4:3

63 Spirit of antichrist

> But every spirit that does not confess Jesus is not from God. This is the spirit of the antichrist, which you have heard is coming; even now it is already in the world.
>
> 1 John 4:3 (CSB)

If the spirit of a prophecy denies Jesus was a human being, it is not from God. If the spirit of a prophecy is rebellious against Jesus, then it is "anti-Christ." The spirit of antichrist has been obvious ever since John's time.

In every generation, people wonder who is the Antichrist? Maybe the most evil leader in the world is the Antichrist. When he dies, they look for someone else. John told us to recognize the spirit of antichrist wherever it comes up. There is much evil in the world today.

> PRAYER: Lord, thank you for warning me about the spirit of antichrist. Amen.

PERSONAL THOUGHTS

1 John 4:4

64 Greater than deception

> You are from God, little children, and you have conquered [false prophets], because the one who is in you is greater than the one who is in the world.
>
> 1 John 4:4 (CSB)

Even immature believers can reject false prophecies. The Holy Spirit in a believer defeats any deception by a spirit of antichrist. A believer can stand for truth in the face of harassment because the Holy Spirit strengthens him.

Whenever I read the news, I notice voices trying to manipulate my opinions. The world's ways are propaganda, trying to convince me to deny Jesus in my life. I can recognize when worldly voices speak with a spirit of antichrist, because I know the Holy Spirit's voice. He is greater than the deception of the world.

> PRAYER: Lord, thank you for the Holy Spirit in me who is greater than the world. Amen.

PERSONAL THOUGHTS

1 John 4:5

65 From the world

> [False prophets] are from the world. Therefore what they say is from the world, and the world listens to them.
>
> 1 John 4:5 (CSB)

If one knows the worldview of prophets, one can see where they are from. A worldly viewpoint results in worldly statements which are embraced by worldly people.

Hardly anyone in public life is a mature Christian. Media commentators, pundits, politicians, and so on are mostly worldly people. So I expect what they say to appeal to unbelievers. It's easy to see why they are popular.

> PRAYER: Lord, thank you for discernment when I read the news. Amen.

PERSONAL THOUGHTS

1 John 4:6

66 Who to listen to

> We are from God. Anyone who knows God listens to us; anyone who is not from God does not listen to us. This is how we know the Spirit of truth and the spirit of deception.
>
> 1 John 4:6 (CSB)

John knew his message was from God. Believers were included when John said, "we." Those who know God listen to John's message and embrace the truth.

I don't listen to preachers on TV anymore. I found too many were appealing to my selfishness. Distinguishing the spirit of truth from the spirit of deception is important for any believer. The Holy Spirit helps me discern which spirit is confronting me.[23]

> PRAYER: Lord, I will listen to those who teach what John is teaching in his letter. Amen.

PERSONAL THOUGHTS

---

[23] 1 Corinthians 12:10.

1 John 4:7

67 Love is from God

> Dear friends, let us love one another, because love is from God, and everyone who loves has been born of God and knows God.
>
> 1 John 4:7 (CSB)

Self-sacrificing love toward believers is a major theme of John's letter. Believers have experienced God's love, because he has forgiven our sins and he cleanses us from unrighteousness. Then God's love is the source of my love for others.

Whenever I've moved my home from one city to another, I've had to find another local church. The most important quality of my new church home is that they love one another. As a visitor, I noticed whether people fellowship before and after a service, what kind of announcements were made, and the depth of my conversations with members. These are clues indicating whether the members love one another.

> PRAYER: Lord, thank you for other believers who love me. Amen.

PERSONAL THOUGHTS

1 John 4:8

68 God is love

> The one who does not love does not know God, because God is love.
> 1 John 4:8 (CSB)

The absence of self-sacrificing love indicates one has not experienced God's love yet. God's essence is love, especially love for people.

When I see people acting selfishly, I don't criticize or judge them. It is usually not my job to correct their behavior. They just need to experience God's love. Perhaps I can find a way to demonstrate God's love. I can also pray that the Lord will reveal himself to them.

> PRAYER: Lord, I know everything you do flows from love. Amen.

PERSONAL THOUGHTS

1 John 4:9

69 Love revealed

God's love was revealed among us in this way: God sent his one and only Son into the world so that we might live through him.

1 John 4:9 (CSB)

God's love for mankind became obvious when he sent Jesus to become a human being who would give up his life on the cross. Whoever believes in him is cleansed of sin and lives through him.[24]

Even in America, most worldly people don't know much about Jesus. I had long conversations with my college friends from non-Christian backgrounds just explaining what Jesus did. It was a start to understanding God's love for them.

> PRAYER: Lord, thank you for sending Jesus so I can understand your love for me. Amen.

PERSONAL THOUGHTS

---

[24] John 3:16.

1 John 4:10

70 Sent his Son

> Love consists in this: not that we loved God, but that he loved us and sent his Son to be the atoning sacrifice for our sins.
>
> 1 John 4:10 (CSB)

God was not responding to mankind's love. He loved us first. God loved us even though we were rebellious. Jesus' death on the cross was necessary to pay for our sins.

I made my commitment to Jesus when I was ten years old. Before then, I was selfish like everyone else. When I realized Jesus died for my sins, I knew I had to change. I have gradually matured as I've learned more and more from the Bible.

> PRAYER: Lord, thank you for sending Jesus before I knew you, when I was naturally selfish. Amen.

PERSONAL THOUGHTS

1 John 4:11

71 We must love

> Dear friends, if God loved us in this way,
> we also must love one another.
>
> 1 John 4:11 (CSB)

Jesus sacrificed himself out of love for us. After experiencing this kind of love, we must love one another with the same kind of love.

Some believers are difficult to love. Recognizing my own selfishness is a first step to loving them. I may have to adjust my attitude toward the difficult ones. Self-sacrificing love means my selfish desires have lower priority than how I can help that difficult believer.

> PRAYER: Lord, help me to love all believers, even the cranky ones. Amen.

PERSONAL THOUGHTS

1 John 4:12

72 Complete love

> No one has ever seen God. If we love one another, God remains in us and his love is made complete in us.
> 1 John 4:12 (CSB)

No one has learned to love by seeing God, but the Holy Spirit who lives in each believer teaches us. Loving one another completes God's purpose.

Loving others requires practical wisdom. I usually don't know what kind of help or encouragement someone needs. I often find the nudges of the Holy Spirit guide me to do simple things for others. I'm surprised by how much they appreciate it, but the Holy Spirit knew.

PRAYER: Lord, let your love shine through me. Amen.

PERSONAL THOUGHTS

1 John 4:13

73   Holy Spirit in us

> This is how we know that we remain in [God] and he in us: He has given us of his Spirit.
>
> 1 John 4:13 (CSB)

The Holy Spirit in us confirms we are in God and he in us.

It is reassuring to know deep down in my soul that I am in God's family. When I mess up and sin by doing something selfish, I wonder what God thinks about me. The Holy Spirit provides assurance and leads me to repent.

> PRAYER: Lord, thank you for the Holy Spirit who gives me assurance of your love. Amen.

PERSONAL THOUGHTS

1 John 4:14

74 God sent a Savior

> And we have seen and we testify that the Father has sent his Son as the world's Savior.
>
> 1 John 4:14 (CSB)

Jesus is the savior for all mankind. Anyone who believes will be saved from the consequences of sin. John witnessed Jesus in person, so this letter tells us what John knows.

Eyewitness accounts about Jesus, like John's gospel, are reliable documentation. I study them so I'm ready with the facts. Over the years, I've met people from around the world and from many different backgrounds. Sometimes they let me tell them about Jesus.

> PRAYER: Lord, help me explain the gospel whenever there is an opportunity. Amen.

PERSONAL THOUGHTS

1 John 4:15

75 Son of God

> Whoever confesses that Jesus is the Son of God—God remains in him and he in God.
>
> 1 John 4:15 (CSB)

Believing in Jesus means one recognizes that he is the Son of God and therefore deserves one's complete loyalty.

Astronomy has confirmed the universe is a big place that began at a moment in time. Discovery after discovery reveal its wonders. The Bible teaches that the Son of God was instrumental in creating the universe.[25] Because Jesus is the Son of God, he is ruler over the entire universe. Therefore, I am completely submitted to his authority.

> PRAYER: Lord, I give my loyalty to Jesus who is the Son of God. Amen.

PERSONAL THOUGHTS

---

[25] John 1:3.

1 John 4:16a

76 Knowing God's love

> And we have come to know and to believe the love that God has for us.
> 1 John 4:16a (CSB)

Having believed that Jesus is the Son of God, I have experienced God's love.

My Christmas gift was a package. As I opened one part, I saw another part yet to be opened and then another and then another.

God's love for me is like a package. I have repented of my sins. I am forgiven. I believe Jesus paid for my sins with his life. He is my savior. I believe he is the Son of God. I am loyal to him. I have the Holy Spirit in me. I am in God's family.

PRAYER: Lord, thank you for letting me experience your love. Amen.

PERSONAL THOUGHTS

1 John 4:16b

77 Remaining in love

> God is love, and the one who remains in love remains in God, and God remains in him.
>
> 1 John 4:16b (CSB)

The essence of God's character is love. Because I belong to him, the Holy Spirit is in me, and my character is being molded into love.

Jesus used the picture of a branch attached to its vine to illustrate remaining in him.[26] A branch gets its life from the vine and produces fruit. God's love gives me the spiritual life necessary to produce love in my actions. As I mature spiritually, God's love becomes embedded in my character more and more.

> PRAYER: Lord, thank you for teaching me to remain in love. Amen.

PERSONAL THOUGHTS

---

[26] John 15:4–5.

1 John 4:17

78   Confidence on judgment day

> In this, love is made complete with us so that we may have confidence in the day of judgment, because as [Jesus] is, so also are we in this world.
>
> 1 John 4:17 (CSB)

On the day of judgment, the heavenly court will be convened. Everyone will be judged for what they have done. Everyone sins, so that sounds very intimidating.

As I experience God's love, I gain confidence that all will be well for me on judgment day.

Jesus died on the cross because of God's love for mankind. That meant I can be forgiven. That fact was the starting point of my walk with God. Because I'm forgiven, judgment day is not intimidating. I will be with Jesus.

> PRAYER: Lord, thank you for giving me confidence regarding judgment day. Amen.

PERSONAL THOUGHTS

1 John 4:18

79 No fear

> There is no fear in love; instead, perfect love drives out fear, because fear involves punishment. So the one who fears is not complete in love.
>
> 1 John 4:18 (CSB)

Having experienced God's love, I am not afraid of God's judgment of sin. I know I have been forgiven, because of his love.

Before I asked Jesus into my life, I was afraid of hell. I tried to earn God's favor by being good—most of the time. When I received God's forgiveness, the fear dissipated. Now, I know God loves me and has cleansed me from sin.

> PRAYER: Lord, thank you for overcoming my fear of punishment. Amen.

PERSONAL THOUGHTS

1 John 4:19

80 Loved first

We love because [God] first loved us.
1 John 4:19 (CSB)

First, I experienced God's love. Then, my natural reaction to being loved is to love him back.

Other world religions don't know about forgiveness, so revenge is the natural reaction to hurts. They haven't experienced God's love yet.

God took the initiative while mankind was entangled in sin. He sent his Son so I can be forgiven. Having experienced his love, I love him and I am able to love others.

> PRAYER: Lord, thank you for loving me first. Amen.

PERSONAL THOUGHTS

1 John 4:20–21

81 Loving whom seen

> If anyone says, "I love God," and yet hates his brother or sister, he is a liar. For the person who does not love his brother or sister whom he has seen cannot love God whom he has not seen. And we have this command from him: The one who loves God must also love his brother and sister.
>
> 1 John 4:20–21 (CSB)

Some people pretend to love God. Hating fellow believers exposes the lie. The one who truly loves God who is spirit, will also love fellow believers who are flesh and blood.

God is a spirit who might seem far away, but brothers and sisters in the Lord affect me directly. They might say or do something I don't like. If I react with anger and hate, I'm not reflecting my love for God. I must control my reactions to show love instead of anger.

> PRAYER: Lord, help me show sincere love to all fellow believers. Amen.

PERSONAL THOUGHTS

1 John 5:1

82 Born of God

> Everyone who believes that Jesus is the Christ has been born of God, and everyone who loves the Father also loves the one born of him.
>
> 1 John 5:1 (CSB)

When one believes Jesus is the Messiah (Christ), the Son of God, submission to his authority naturally follows. The result is being spiritually born into God's family. When I love the head of God's family, the Father, then I love everyone else in his family too.

When I believed in Jesus, I was relieved to know I was destined for heaven. That was the start of my adventure loving the Father and learning to show love toward other believers in a practical way.

> PRAYER: Lord, I believe Jesus is the Messiah. Amen.

PERSONAL THOUGHTS

1 John 5:2–3

83 Obeying God's commands

> This is how we know that we love God's children: when we love God and obey his commands. For this is what love for God is: to keep his commands. And his commands are not a burden.
>
> 1 John 5:2–3 (CSB)

Jesus said the greatest commandment in the Old Testament is to love God.[27] My love for God is expressed in action by doing what he says to do. Loving his children is one of the important things he wants me to do.

My computer seems to be bossy. It keeps commanding me to do this or that. Obeying computer commands helps avoid bigger problems later. Obeying commands is part of life.

The Bible, especially the New Testament, teaches me how to live in a way that pleases God. Keeping my attitude clean and avoiding selfishness are where I start. Loving God with all my heart, soul, and mind makes everything else easy.

> PRAYER: Lord, help me obey your commands. Amen.

PERSONAL THOUGHTS

---

[27] Matthew 22:36–38.

84 Victory

> Everyone who has been born of God conquers the world. This is the victory that has conquered the world: our faith.
> 1 John 5:4 (CSB)

Members of God's family have the power to overcome the world's influence in life. Faith energizes my victory over the world.

There is a struggle in life between the world and God's kingdom. The world tries to make me conform to its ungodly patterns. But I am not a citizen of this world system. I am in God's family, so I don't have to live by the world's standards. My faith in Jesus is why I have victory over the world's influence.

> PRAYER: Lord, thank you for victory over the world. Amen.

PERSONAL THOUGHTS

1 John 5:5

85 Conquerer

> Who is the one who conquers the world but the one who believes that Jesus is the Son of God?
>
> 1 John 5:5 (CSB)

Believing Jesus is the Son of God makes God's power available to me. Then I am equipped to effectively resist the world's influence in my life.

Jesus healed the sick and cast out demons. He demonstrated his power over Satan. He rose from the dead. He is more powerful than death. He has delegated his authority to believers and promised eternal life. I often pray for the sick and resist demons when necessary. Satan and the world can't threaten me.

> PRAYER: Lord, thank you for making me a conquerer. Amen.

PERSONAL THOUGHTS

1 John 5:6–8

86 Confirmation

> Jesus Christ—he is the one who came by water and blood, not by water only, but by water and by blood. And the Spirit is the one who testifies, because the Spirit is the truth. For there are three that testify: the Spirit, the water, and the blood—and these three are in agreement.
>
> 1 John 5:6–8 (CSB)

It is not clear what John meant by the phrase "by water and blood." Ever since the early church fathers, commentators have speculated about what he meant.[28] However, it is clear that the Holy Spirit confirms that Jesus is the Messiah, the Son of God.

In court, truth is confirmed by the testimony of witnesses. I believe the most reliable witness of all, the Holy Spirit, who always speaks the truth.

> PRAYER: Lord, thank you for the Holy Spirit's confirmation about Jesus. Amen.

PERSONAL THOUGHTS

---

[28]Barker, "1 John," p. 350.

1 John 5:9–10a

87 Testimony

> If we accept human testimony, God's testimony is greater, because it is God's testimony that he has given about his Son. The one who believes in the Son of God has this testimony within himself.
> 1 John 5:9–10a (CSB)

In court, a jury usually believes human witnesses because they swear to tell the truth. God is more truthful than any human, so we know his testimony about Jesus is true.

During Jesus' ministry on earth, God testified that Jesus is the Son. For example, at Jesus' baptism, the Holy Spirit landed on him in the form of a dove. On the Mount of Transfiguration, John heard the Father say Jesus is his Son. Each believer has the Holy Spirit within confirming Jesus is the Son of God.

> PRAYER: Lord, I believe God's testimony about Jesus. Amen.

PERSONAL THOUGHTS

1 John 5:10b

88 Rejecting testimony

> The one who does not believe God has made him a liar, because he has not believed in the testimony God has given about his Son.
>
> 1 John 5:10b (CSB)

If someone rejects the truth of God's testimony about Jesus, he is essentially calling God a liar. God always speaks the truth.

Sometimes a witness in court lies to the jury. When I'm on a jury, I evaluate the witness's character. Is he an honest person or an inveterate liar? Does his story line up with true things I know? Unlike fallible people, I know God always tells the truth, so what he says about Jesus is true. Jesus is the Son of God.

> PRAYER: Lord, I know you always speak the truth. Amen.

PERSONAL THOUGHTS

1 John 5:11–12

89 Life in Jesus

> And this is the testimony: God has given us eternal life, and this life is in his Son. The one who has the Son has life. The one who does not have the Son of God does not have life.
>
> 1 John 5:11–12 (CSB)

Life in Jesus is evidence that Jesus is the Son of God. Because of Jesus, I have eternal life.

God's testimony about Jesus isn't just words. He has given life to all who believe in Jesus, including me. Life in Jesus is more than just existing. It is full and free from the bondage of sin. Moreover, I have the promise of eternal life with him forever.

> PRAYER: Lord, thank you for life in Jesus. Amen.

PERSONAL THOUGHTS

1 John 5:13

90 Eternal life

> I have written these things to you who believe in the name of the Son of God so that you may know that you have eternal life.
>
> 1 John 5:13 (CSB)

John's motivation for writing this letter was to assure believers that they have eternal life. I am a believer, so his letter is personally addressed to me.

John personally knew Jesus. When he wrote this letter, he had had a lifetime of experience as an apostle. I can trust what he says about Jesus. I don't need to worry about the future. I have eternal life.

> PRAYER: Lord, thank you for inspiring John to write his letter for me. Amen.

PERSONAL THOUGHTS

1 John 5:14

91   Confidence in prayer

> This is the confidence we have before [God]: If we ask anything according to his will, he hears us.
>
> 1 John 5:14 (CSB)

As a member of God's family, I am sure he hears my requests when I ask for something that is consistent with his character.

Of course, God won't support my sinful behavior. He won't give me something harmful even if I ask for it. But the heavenly Father is generous toward his children. He wants to listen to me even though I have an incomplete understanding of a situation. My prayers are important to him.

PRAYER: Lord, thank you for hearing my prayers. Amen.

PERSONAL THOUGHTS

1 John 5:15

92   Answers to prayer

> And if we know that [God] hears whatever we ask, we know that we have what we have asked of him.
> 1 John 5:15 (CSB)

God patiently listens to my prayers. I am confident that he grants my requests that are consistent with his character.

When I hear about difficult situations, I pray right away. Perhaps someone is sick, or someone needs other help. I usually don't know the details. I tell God about the situations and present my requests. I can trust him to work things out in a wonderful way for me and others who are involved.

> PRAYER: Lord, thank you for answering my prayers. Amen.

PERSONAL THOUGHTS

1 John 5:16a

93 Intercession for believers

> If anyone sees a fellow believer committing a sin that doesn't lead to death, he should ask, and God will give life to him—to those who commit sin that doesn't lead to death.
>
> 1 John 5:16a (CSB)

Intercession in prayer for fellow believers is important, especially when I see a fellow believer sinning. I will pray. God will answer.

Intercession in prayer for such a believer is helpful, because God will work in the sinning believer's life to bring him to repentance. Repentance and confession to God are the solution for sin.[29]

> PRAYER: Lord, I will pray earnestly for fellow believers. Amen.

PERSONAL THOUGHTS

---

[29] 1 John 1:9.

1 John 5:16b–17

94 Deadly sin

> There is sin that leads to death. I am not saying he should pray about that. All unrighteousness is sin, and there is sin that doesn't lead to death.
>
> 1 John 5:16b–17 (CSB)

John does not explain which sins lead to death, so commentators have speculated ever since the early church fathers. Because I don't know which sins lead to death, I will pray for restoration of any believer I see in sin.

John is clear that sin is not excusable. For example, there is no such thing as a "white lie." Lying is just sin. People pretend that common sins are okay, but they are just fooling themselves.

> PRAYER: Lord, I recognize all unrighteousness is sin. Amen.

PERSONAL THOUGHTS

1 John 5:18

95 Not sinning

> We know that everyone who has been born of God does not sin, but the one who is born of God keeps himself, and the evil one does not touch him.
>
> 1 John 5:18 (CSB)

Those in God's family do not sin habitually, because they are careful to do what pleases the Father. Satan doesn't have influence over them like he does over people in the world.

I can resist temptation to sin by God's power in me. Doing what God wants is my highest priority. Living like my worldly friends is not enticing at all. I found out my friends' worldly parties were just boring.

> PRAYER: Lord, thank you for freeing me from habitual sin. Amen.

PERSONAL THOUGHTS

1 John 5:19

96   Evil one

> We know that we are of God, and the whole world is under the sway of the evil one.
>
> 1 John 5:19 (CSB)

Satan has influence over people in the world. Sinners want to sin, so temptation, corruption, and destruction are easy for Satan.

I've observed that in the world a little sin here and a little sin there adds up to a big evil result. For example, greed is very common. If many people are just a little greedy, the result is poverty destroying its victims. The world may be influenced by Satan, but I don't have to be.

> PRAYER: Lord, help me recognize Satan's influence in this world. Amen.

PERSONAL THOUGHTS

1 John 5:20

97 True God

> And we know that the Son of God has come and has given us understanding so that we may know the true one. We are in the true one—that is, in his Son, Jesus Christ. He is the true God and eternal life.
>
> 1 John 5:20 (CSB)

Jesus revealed the heavenly Father by what he did here on earth. By faith, I am in him and he is in me. There no other one who is God.

Religions of the world have many ideas about who is God. False gods don't compare to Jesus who rose from the dead. Jesus is the Messiah and Son of God. And by the way, he has given me eternal life.

> PRAYER: Lord, thank you for sending Jesus, so I can know the one true God. Amen.

PERSONAL THOUGHTS

1 John 5:21

98 No idols

> Little children, guard yourselves from idols.
>
> 1 John 5:21 (csb)

Those in God's family know the true God and so must not be seduced to worship idols.

Modern society has idols just like ancient peoples. Some people worship money, some fame, some sports, and some political power. For example, I went to a major college football game. There was a huge investment of time and money. The crowd was dedicated to their team, and in the tailgate area, I could smell the smoke of burnt offerings. The sport was like an idol to some.

> Prayer: Lord, help me recognize idols in modern society. Amen.

personal thoughts

Meditations on 2 John

This second letter is addressed to a "lady and her children." It is unclear whether this was a specific person, or more likely, a metaphor for a local church and its members.

2 John 1:1–2

99 Eternal truth

> The elder:
> To the elect lady and her children, whom I love in the truth—and not only I, but also all who know the truth—because of the truth that remains in us and will be with us forever.
> 2 John 1:1–2 (CSB)

This letter is addressed to a "lady and her children." The church has embraced this letter from the beginning, so its message is for me.

Truth about Jesus is a theme of John's letters, almost as a synonym for the gospel. John loved believers who know the truth which will last forever.

When I was in high school, I saw a cover of *Time* magazine (1966) that said "Is God dead?" Inside was an article about Death-of-God theology. I could tell those theologians did not have the truth in them. Jesus said his words would last forever.[30] I cling to the gospel message and it will be part of me forever.

> PRAYER: Lord, like John, I love fellow believers who cling to the truth about you. Amen.

PERSONAL THOUGHTS

---

[30] Matthew 24:35.

100 Grace, mercy, and peace

> Grace, mercy, and peace will be with us from God the Father and from Jesus Christ, the Son of the Father, in truth and love.
>
> 2 John 1:3 (CSB)

The blessings of grace, mercy, and peace are from from God the Father and from Jesus, the Messiah, the Son of God.

I felt like I was walking on clouds the night I believed in Jesus. I had his peace. God has forgiven my sins and cleaned me up. His motive was his grace and mercy. As a result I have peace in my soul because sin no longer has me in its grip.

> PRAYER: Lord, thank you for the grace, mercy, and peace you have given me. Amen.

PERSONAL THOUGHTS

2 John 1:4

101 Walking in truth

> I was very glad to find some of your children walking in truth, in keeping with a command we have received from the Father.
>
> 2 John 1:4 (CSB)

John had heard about believers who where doing what God has commanded, to walk in the truth of the gospel, namely, to walk in love.

Like John, I am happy to see believers express their love for each other. It might be wise counsel, a helping hand, or just a hug. I keep finding examples of how to love in the Bible. The more I practice loving others, the easier it becomes.

> PRAYER: Lord, I will keep living according to the way taught by your Word. Amen.

PERSONAL THOUGHTS

2 John 1:5

102 Reminder

> So now I ask you, dear lady—not as if I were writing you a new command, but one we have had from the beginning—that we love one another.
>
> 2 John 1:5 (CSB)

John reminded the recipients of his letter to love one another. This was not a new requirement. Jesus taught us to love other believers.

Some people irritate me. Some people have mistaken ideas. Some people are manipulative. Some people are always critical of others. It is harder to love such people even though they are believers. Jesus didn't give me any loopholes. I have to love.

PRAYER: Lord, thank you for the reminder to love other believers. Amen.

PERSONAL THOUGHTS

2 John 1:6

103 Walking in love

> This is love: that we walk according to his commands. This is the command as you have heard it from the beginning: that you walk in love.
>
> 2 John 1:6 (CSB)

Jesus' teaching and his example showed how to walk in love. He sacrificed his life, so we can be cleansed from sin.

Taking a walk in my neighborhood is a chance to walk in love. I get to give a friendly wave to strangers. I get to scratch dogs and greet the masters. I get to visit with neighbors. Sometimes I get to pray for someone in need.

Love is not just a one time event. I must love continuously. I must love all kinds of people. Each action must be based on love. Throughout the day, I must examine my motives. Living an unselfish lifestyle is the starting point for walking in love.

> PRAYER: Lord, living in love will be my highest priority. Amen.

PERSONAL THOUGHTS

104 Many deceivers

> Many deceivers have gone out into the world; they do not confess the coming of Jesus Christ in the flesh. This is the deceiver and the antichrist.
>
> 2 John 1:7 (CSB)

In John's time, some who claimed to be Christians said Jesus was not a human being. John warned believers about them. Even today, some deny who Jesus is with sophisticated sounding arguments.

Propaganda is overflowing in the media these days. That's what non-Christians do. They try to manipulate public opinion. False doctrine has seeped into the church today, too. I must carefully compare teaching to what the Bible says. John's warning is true today.

> PRAYER: Lord, thank you for warning me about deceivers. Amen.

PERSONAL THOUGHTS

2 John 1:8

105 Watch

> Watch yourselves so that you don't lose what we have worked for, but that you may receive a full reward.
>
> 2 John 1:8 (CSB)

John cautioned believers to not let deceivers destroy their faith. Believers must maintain a godly lifestyle which God will reward.

When I was in college, some members of my adult Sunday School class advocated popular ideas. Then I realized they didn't believe the Bible.

I must assess my own faith, so deceivers don't corrupt me. Then I will be equipped to help others remain strong in the faith, so we will receive the rewards God has prepared for those who love him.

PRAYER: Lord, I will be careful to not be deceived by false believers. Amen.

PERSONAL THOUGHTS

106 Going beyond

> Anyone who does not remain in Christ's teaching but goes beyond it does not have God. The one who remains in that teaching, this one has both the Father and the Son.
>
> 2 John 1:9 (CSB)

John warned that some false teachers were going beyond what Jesus taught, teaching their own ideas. Those who are true to the faith are careful to teach what Jesus said and no more.

When a Scripture passage is vague or ambiguous it is tempting to guess what it means instead of saying, "I don't know." I've heard some preachers take a small verse out of context and weave elaborate symbolism from it. John warned me to not follow such.

PRAYER: Lord, help me recognize speculation in Bible studies. Amen.

PERSONAL THOUGHTS

2 John 1:10–11

107 Hospitality

> If anyone comes to you and does not bring this teaching, do not receive him into your home, and do not greet him; for the one who greets him shares in his evil works.
>
> 2 John 1:10–11 (CSB)

In John's time, it was common to host traveling evangelists in a believer's home. However, John warned believers to evaluate what the teacher was saying before extending hospitality.

Hospitality is a Christian virtue, but I need to know who I might host. A recommendation from a wise friend who knows the visitor helps. Today, the Internet often allows me to see for myself what a visitor is teaching. The Holy Spirit helps me sense whether there are any "red flags." Hospitality is a way to express love to other believers. However, I must be careful who I invite in.

> PRAYER: Lord, help me discern who is worthy of hospitality. Amen.

PERSONAL THOUGHTS

2 John 1:12–13

108 Greetings from far away

> Though I have many things to write to you, I don't want to use paper and ink. Instead, I hope to come to you and talk face to face so that our joy may be complete.
>
> The children of your elect sister send you greetings.
>
> 2 John 1:12–13 (CSB)

John concluded his letter with a personal note. He knew that fellowshipping in person brings more joy than a letter. John also conveyed greetings from believers near him.

When my wife and I visited China, we told the believers in a home Bible study that our church in Florida was praying specifically for them in their city. The Chinese believers were touched by love from half way around the world.

> PRAYER: Lord, show me how my letters can express your love for believers across the distances. Amen.

PERSONAL THOUGHTS

Meditations on 3 John

This third letter was addressed to Gaius. *Gaius* was a common name in the Roman world. We do not know anything about this Gaius except what is in this letter.

3 John 1:1–2

109 Prospering

> The elder:
>
> To my dear friend Gaius, whom I love in the truth.
>
> Dear friend, I pray that you are prospering in every way and are in good health, just as your whole life is going well, as your soul prospers.[31]
>
> 3 John 1:1–2 (CSB)

This third letter is addressed to Gaius, a friend of John. However, I can apply its message to my life as well.

John prayed for Gaius's prosperity. Prosperity is much more than financial well being. It includes physical health, soul health, and spiritual health.

From time to time, my wife and I hear that a friend has a chronic health problem or other special need. Jesus taught us to pray persistently. So, each morning after breakfast, we pray for each person by name. Like John, I will pray for the whole package of prosperity for my friends.

> PRAYER: Lord, prosper my fellow believers with your provision, health, soul well being, and spiritual blessings. Amen.

---

[31] Quoting the footnote of the *Christian Standard Bible* for clarity.

110 Fidelity

> For I was very glad when fellow believers came and testified to your fidelity to the truth—how you are walking in truth.
>
> 3 John 1:3 (CSB)

Apparently, some believers had visited Gaius, seen how he was living, and then gave John a report. John was pleased to learn that Gaius' life was faithful to the gospel.

When the label on a vinyl record says "high fidelity," it is claiming to reproduce the music to sound just like a live performance. I want my life to be just like the Word of God says it should, to show fidelity to the truth. Gaius is a good example for any believer today.

> PRAYER: Lord, help me live with fidelity to your Word. Amen.

PERSONAL THOUGHTS

/ 3 John 1:4

111 Children walking

> I have no greater joy than this: to hear that my children are walking in truth.
>
> 3 John 1:4 (CSB)

A father is thrilled when he sees his baby take his first steps. You will hear encouragement, "Come to Papa." John felt the same way when he found out Gaius was living the way he had been taught. John considered those who became believers under his supervision to be like his own children.

Jesus said, "I am the way, the truth, and the life."[32] Living in truth means living the Jesus way. The Bible teaches me what his lifestyle means. The Holy Spirit helps me avoid sin and do what the Bible teaches.

PRAYER: Lord, help me walk in truth. Amen.

PERSONAL THOUGHTS

---

[32] John 14:6 (KJV).

3 John 1:5

112 Faithful hospitality

> Dear friend, you are acting faithfully in whatever you do for the brothers and sisters, especially when they are strangers.
>
> 3 John 1:5 (CSB)

Apparently, Gaius received visitors from John and showed them hospitality, even though Gaius had not met them before. In his earlier letter, John had warned about receiving false teachers.[33] The visitors from John were genuine believers.

When my wife and I visited Malaysia, local church members gave us fellowship, meals, and a place to sleep. We were thankful for their hospitality.

Hospitality for fellow believers is a way I can show self-sacrificing love. Each believer is able to help in his own way. A loving attitude is what is important, which motivates appropriate action.

> PRAYER: Lord, help me discern the hospitality I should provide genuine believers. Amen.

PERSONAL THOUGHTS

---

[33] 2 John 1:10.

3 John 1:6–7

113 Supporting evangelists

> [Fellow believers] have testified to your love before the church. You will do well to send them on their journey in a manner worthy of God, since they set out for the sake of the Name, accepting nothing from pagans.
>
> 3 John 1:6–7 (CSB)

Apparently, the visitors from John were itinerant evangelists. John recommended that Gaius send the visitors on their way with support.

I can follow the example of Gaius. Whenever I recognize how an evangelistic team is contributing to the spread of the gospel, I can help support their ministry. Generosity is one way love for believers is put into action.

> PRAYER: Lord, show me my part in supporting itinerant ministries that I encounter. Amen.

PERSONAL THOUGHTS

114 Coworkers

> Therefore, we ought to support such people so that we can be coworkers with the truth.
>
> 3 John 1:8 (CSB)

By supporting the ministries of other believers, we become indirect coworkers with them in spreading the gospel.

From the beginning, my wife and I have financially supported several mission organizations and individuals on a regular basis. From time to time, we have given to others who we encountered or who visited our church. We felt like coworkers with them.

> PRAYER: Lord, thank you for allowing me to be a coworker with those who spread the gospel. Amen.

PERSONAL THOUGHTS

3 John 1:9

115 Loving first place

> I wrote something to the church, but Diotrephes, who loves to have first place among them, does not receive our authority.
>
> 3 John 1:9 (CSB)

Apparently, Diotrephes was a leader of a local group of Christians. Due to pride, he resisted guidance from John who was a recognized apostle.

Holding an office in an organization strokes one's pride. I've had to repent when I wanted a higher role in a Christian organization. Ambition to have first place is a trap. Submitting to the spiritual authority of more mature believers has helped me avoid that trap.

> PRAYER: Lord, help me avoid the pride of wanting to be in first place. Amen.

PERSONAL THOUGHTS

3 John 1:10

116 Refusing hospitality

> This is why, if I come, I will remind [Diotrephes] of the works he is doing, slandering us with malicious words. And he is not satisfied with that! He not only refuses to welcome fellow believers, but he even stops those who want to do so and expels them from the church.
>
> 3 John 1:10 (CSB)

John promised to discipline Diotrephes when he visits that area in person. The pride of Diotrephes led to further sin when he refused to give hospitality.

Whenever my church had a visiting preacher, frequently with his wife, the church office arranged for a big fruit basket and flowers to be delivered to their hotel room. It was a special effort to be hospitable. When I welcome fellow believers, I am demonstrating the unity in Christ that Jesus wants us to have.

> PRAYER: Lord, help me find ways to show unity among believers. Amen.

PERSONAL THOUGHTS

3 John 1:11

117 Imitating good

> Dear friend, do not imitate what is evil, but what is good. The one who does good is of God; the one who does evil has not seen God.
>
> 3 John 1:11 (CSB)

John advised Gaius to imitate what is good and not the example of Diotrephes. Doing good is evidence that one belongs to God's family.

I have grown gradually as a Christian. Along the way, there have been mature believers I have looked up to. I have learned both spiritual and practical lessons just by observing how they lived. I saw how they handled the difficult times in life and how they rejoiced in the good times. I am thankful for them.

> PRAYER: Lord, help me imitate the good examples among my fellow believers. Amen.

PERSONAL THOUGHTS

118 Good reputation

> Everyone speaks well of Demetrius — even the truth itself. And we also speak well of him, and you know that our testimony is true.
>
> 3 John 1:12 (CSB)

John commended Demetrius. He had a good reputation, and apparently, John knew him.

Angie told me about a special couple who had helped her as a new believer. The wife came across the country to be in our wedding. A few years later, I got to know them both when we visited California. They had a good reputation.

> PRAYER: Lord, thank you for fellow believers who have a good reputation. Amen.

PERSONAL THOUGHTS

3 John 1:13–14

119   Face to face

> I have many things to write you, but I don't want to write to you with pen and ink. I hope to see you soon, and we will talk face to face.
>
> 3 John 1:13–14 (CSB)

Like his second letter, John concluded with a personal note. Letters could not convey all John wanted to share with Gaius. Meeting face to face was necessary.

My wife and I visited the church we were married in for the first time in twenty-three years. We hugged necks and had lunch with a dear couple who had been in a home Bible study with us twenty-five years before. Letters cannot substitute for face to face fellowship.

> PRAYER: Lord, thank you for opportunities to meet with dear friends face to face. Amen.

PERSONAL THOUGHTS

3 John 1:15

120 Friends

> Peace to you. The friends send you greetings. Greet the friends by name.
> 3 John 1:15 (CSB)

John gave Gaius a blessing of peace. The believers with John sent their greetings to Gaius and his friends.

Before the Internet, I sent paper letters of greetings and news to friends each Christmastime. Now, email has replaced paper letters and social media has enabled contact over great distances. As we spend time together, relationships with other believers develop into lifelong friendships.

> PRAYER: Lord, thank you for friends in God's family. Amen.

Index

Advocate, 12
agapao (*Strong's* No. 25), 19
Already received, 18
Anointing, 31
Answers to prayer, 93
Assurance, 58
Atoning sacrifice, 13

Believing, 60
Belonging, 30
Bible reference
   Genesis
      4:1–16, 52
   Leviticus
      19:18, 60
   Matthew
      5:21–22, 55
      6:33, 26
      7:21–23, 44
      22:36–38, 84
      24:35, 102
   John
      1:3, 76
      3:16, 70
      5:24, 36
      13:34, 19, 60
      13:34–35, 51
      14:6, 116
      15:4–5, 17, 78
      15:5, 35
   Romans
      3:23, 11
      8:1, 17
   1 Corinthians
      12:10, 62, 67
      13:4–5, 57
      15:49–54, 42
   Hebrews
      4:15, 45
   1 John
      1:1, 2
      1:2, 3
      1:3, 4
      1:4, 5
      1:5, 6
      1:6, 7
      1:7, 8
      1:8, 9
      1:9, 10, 94
      1:10, 11

Index

2:1, 12
2:2, 13
2:3, 14
2:4, 15
2:5, 16
2:5–6, 17
2:7, 18
2:8, 19
2:9, 20
2:10, 21
2:11, 22
2:12–14, 23
2:13–14, 24, 25
2:15, 26
2:16, 27
2:17, 28
2:18, 29
2:19, 30
2:20, 31
2:21, 32
2:22, 33
2:23, 34
2:24, 35
2:25, 36
2:26, 37
2:27, 38
2:28, 39
2:29, 40
3:1, 41
3:2, 42
3:3, 43
3:4, 44
3:5, 45

3:6, 46
3:7, 47
3:8, 48
3:9, 49
3:10, 50
3:11, 51
3:12, 52
3:13, 53
3:14, 54
3:15, 55
3:16, 56
3:17–18, 57
3:19–20, 58
3:21–22, 59
3:23, 60
3:24, 61
4:1, 62
4:2, 63
4:3, 64
4:4, 65
4:5, 66
4:6, 67
4:7, 68
4:8, 69
4:9, 70
4:10, 71
4:11, 72
4:12, 73
4:13, 74
4:14, 75
4:15, 76
4:16a, 77
4:16b, 78

Index

4:17, 79
4:18, 80
4:19, 81
4:20–21, 82
5:1, 83
5:2–3, 84
5:4, 85
5:5, 86
5:6–8, 87
5:9–10a, 88
5:10b, 89
5:11–12, 90
5:13, 91
5:14, 92
5:15, 93
5:16a, 94
5:16b–17, 95
5:18, 96
5:19, 97
5:20, 98
5:21, 99
2 John
  1:1–2, 102
  1:3, 103
  1:4, 104
  1:5, 105
  1:6, 106
  1:7, 107
  1:8, 108
  1:9, 109
  1:10, 117
  1:10–11, 110
  1:12–13, 111

3 John
  1:1–2, 114
  1:3, 115
  1:4, 116
  1:5, 117
  1:6–7, 118
  1:8, 119
  1:9, 120
  1:10, 121
  1:11, 122
  1:12, 123
  1:13–14, 124
  1:15, 125
Revelation
  12:11, 25
Blind, 22
Born of God, 83

Children walking, 116
Complete love, 73
Confessing the Son, 34
Confidence, 59
Confidence in prayer, 92
Confidence on judgment day, 79
Confirmation, 87
Conquerer, 86
Coworkers, 119

Deadly sin, 95
Deceived, 9

Index

Deceivers, 37
Denying Jesus, 33
Desiring the world, 27
Destroying the devil's works, 48
Does not keep on sinning, 46
Doing right, 40

Eternal life, 91
Eternal truth, 102
Eternity, 36
Evil one, 97

Face to face, 124
Faithful hospitality, 117
Fellowship, 4
Fidelity, 115
Forgiven, 10
Friends, 125
From death to life, 54
From the world, 66

God's children, 41
God is love, 69
God sent a Savior, 75
Going beyond, 109
Good reputation, 123
Grace, mercy, and peace, 103
Greater than deception, 65

Greetings from far away, 111

Hated by the world, 53
Holy Spirit in us, 74
Hospitality, 110
How to know God, 14

Imitating good, 122
Intercession for believers, 94
In the dark, 20
In the light, 21

Jesus' new command, 19
Joy, 5

Knowing God's love, 77
Knowing the truth, 32

Lawlessness, 44
Life in Jesus, 90
Light, 6
Like him, 42
Loved first, 81
Love in action, 57
Love is from God, 68
Love made complete, 16
Love one another, 51
Love revealed, 70
Loving first place, 120

Index

Loving the world, 26
Loving whom seen, 82

Many antichrists, 29
Many deceivers, 107
Murder, 55

No fear, 80
No idols, 99
Not ashamed, 39
Not practicing sin, 49
Not sinning, 96

Obeying God's commands, 84

Pretending to know God, 15
Prospering, 114
Purified, 43

Refusing hospitality, 121
Rejecting testimony, 89
Remaining, 61
Remaining in love, 78
Reminder, 105
Righteous, 47

Selfless love, 56
Sent his Son, 71
Sinner, 11
Son of God, 76

Spirit of antichrist, 64
Spirit of God, 63
Supporting evangelists, 118

Taking away sin, 45
Taught by the anointing, 38
Temporary desires, 28
Testimony, 88
Testing spirits, 62
The devil's children, 50
The Word remaining, 35
To fathers, 24
To little children, 23
To young men, 25
True God, 98
Truth, 2

Unlike Cain, 52

Victory, 85

Walking, 17
Walking in darkness, 7
Walking in light, 8
Walking in love, 106
Walking in truth, 104
Watch, 108
We must love, 72

Index

Who to listen to, 67
Word of life, 3

About the author

Edward B. Allen is the author of books for three styles of devotional Bible study. Verse-by-verse books draw devotional points from the Scripture passage in sequence. Historical-people books focus on incidents in the lives of historical people that illustrate biblical principles. Topical books explore relevant Scriptures throughout the Bible. His books also include many personal stories from modern life.

His books are in two series. Books in the *A Slow Walk* series have short meditations in daily-devotional format, such as *A Slow Walk through Psalm 119: 90 Devotional Meditations*. Books in the *Devotional Commentary* series are straight reads with a devotional slant, rather than academic or theological comments, such as *Practical Faith: A Devotional Commentary*.

He has led discussion Bible-study groups in evangelical churches for over 50 years He received a Ph.D. in Computer Science degree at Florida Atlantic University and had a career in software engineering. He has authored or coauthored over 80 professional papers.

www.ingramcontent.com/pod-product-compliance
Lightning Source LLC
Chambersburg PA
CBHW060834050426
42453CB00008B/684